ANGELA McAL

NOTHING TO DO

THE BODLEY HEAD
LONDON

For William
with love

With many thanks to Mary Plumridge,
Ginny Westwood and Sue Witt

British Library Cataloguing in Publication Data

McAllister, Angela
Nothing to do.
1. Activities for pre-school children – For children
I. Title
790.1'922

ISBN 0-370-31259-7

Copyright © Angela McAllister 1989
Printed and bound in Hong Kong for
The Bodley Head Ltd,
32 Bedford Square, London WC1B 3SG
First published 1989

CONTENTS

Messing About with Boats	5
Jigsaws	6
Mad Misfits	7
Yogophones	8
Finger Puppets	9
Green Fingers	10
Skittles	12
Painted Pasta	13
Rogues' Gallery	14
A Spinning Dice	15
Snakes and Ladders	16
Pom-poms	18
Lanterns	19
Magic Paintings	20
Creepy Crawlies	21
Snap!	22
Flour Pictures	23
Finger and Footprints	24
String Painting	25
It's Sew Easy!	26
Rubbings	27
Feeling Fancy	28
Plasticine Printing	29
Let's Pretend . . .	30
Bits and Bobs	32

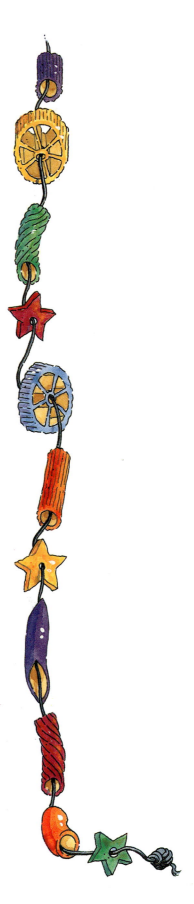

INTRODUCTION

There are inevitably moments when the most contented young child asks, 'What can I do *now*?' and when the most resourceful adult runs short of ideas. *Nothing To Do* is my answer at those moments. But I hope it offers more than just ways to occupy a bored child for half an hour (although that in itself may save somebody's sanity!). The ideas in it are designed to develop hand–eye coordination, to suggest games, to inspire 'let's pretend', and to stimulate that most valuable natural resource on any wet afternoon – your child's and your imagination.

   I have been careful to use materials that are inexpensive and available (things you might easily have in the house), and at the back of the book there are recipes for simple essentials: paste and papier mâché. You should always use round-ended scissors, and protect all surfaces generously with newspaper. If paint or glue is involved, adults and children should 'dress for mess' – an old shirt will do if you haven't got an overall.

   All activities must be supervised, but more importantly they should be shared. Children only learn if they try . . . and if they are enjoying themselves.

MESSING ABOUT WITH BOATS

Cut a plastic or polystyrene egg carton in half. The lid will make a flat-bottomed boat. If there are any holes, plug them up with Plasticine. The bottom can be cut lengthways or widthways to make smaller boats. Fix a straw or pencil mast into the boat with a blob of Plasticine. Cut out a paper sail, decorate it using pencils or paints and tape to the mast. Tape a piece of wool or string at the front to pull the boat along with.

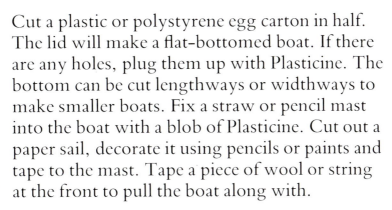

Load the boat with cargo – buttons, dried beans or pasta for a freighter, toy farm or zoo animals for Noah's Ark, or to carry the soap at bathtime.

Give your boat a name . . . and launch it!

JIGSAWS

Cut out two identical, simple and clear pictures from magazines. (Advertisements are easy to find repeated.) Glue the back of one picture all over with flour and water paste (see p. 32) and stick it on to a piece of card. Cut into large pieces with straight or wavy lines.
Jumble them up and then . . . try to put them back together again! Keep the pieces in a strong envelope together with the second picture for reference.

MAD MISFITS

Roughly cut pieces of people from magazines – the crazier the better. Then stick the pieces on to a sheet of paper with flour and water paste (see p. 32) to make mad misfit people. Use the face from an old photograph of a relative or friend and stick on to a misfit body for a funny birthday card.

Don't forget misfit pets . . .

YOGOPHONES

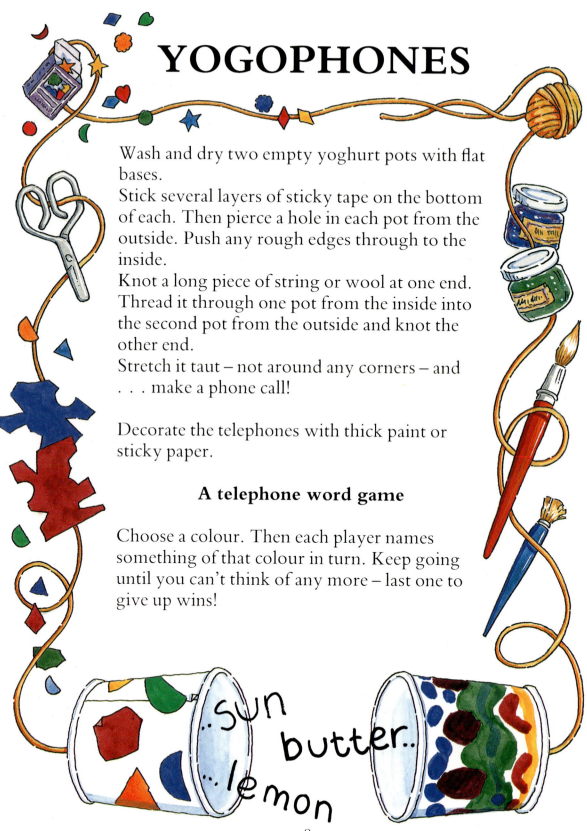

Wash and dry two empty yoghurt pots with flat bases.
Stick several layers of sticky tape on the bottom of each. Then pierce a hole in each pot from the outside. Push any rough edges through to the inside.
Knot a long piece of string or wool at one end. Thread it through one pot from the inside into the second pot from the outside and knot the other end.
Stretch it taut – not around any corners – and . . . make a phone call!

Decorate the telephones with thick paint or sticky paper.

A telephone word game

Choose a colour. Then each player names something of that colour in turn. Keep going until you can't think of any more – last one to give up wins!

FINGER PUPPETS

Cut a semi-circle of stiff paper or card, about 7 cm in diameter. Curl into a cone around the finger and tape. Put a blob of Plasticine on the end of your finger to hold it on. Then decorate. It is easier to do this while it's on your finger.

Give a shaggy dog a straggly wool or string coat.

Stick pink paper ears and wool or cotton whiskers on a little white mouse.

Draw a witch's face. Give it a black hat and spiky wool hair.

Draw a clown's face. Give it a pom-pom hat using coloured cotton wool or pencils. Or cut a face from a magazine and stick it on.

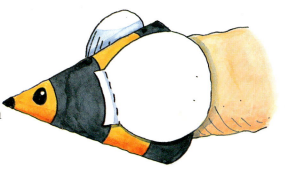

Give a bee a stripy body and wings. Add wings for a bird or a plane too.

GREEN FINGERS

All sorts of pips and seeds can be planted in jam jars – or even sneaked into the pots of other plants.

Planting

Place pebbles, for drainage, at the bottom of a jam jar or flower pot, then half fill with compost. Drop in pips, spaced apart, cover with about 2 cm of compost and water gently. If using a jam jar, fix a piece of polythene over the rim with an elastic band. If using a flower pot, put the pot in a polythene bag and secure with a knot or elastic band. Put in a warm place, water gently, keep moist and watch carefully.

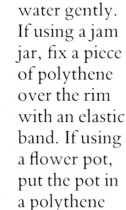

Fruit

Try oranges, tangerines, mandarins, grapefruit, lemons, which take three to four weeks to germinate on average. Or apples and pears which take three to eight weeks. As soon as pips produce two open leaves, carefully lift them with a fork and plant in individual pots.

Do not expect every pip to grow – but keep planting and watching and you should produce a seedling.

Beans

Soak a couple of dried beans in tepid water for a day. Put a piece of blotting paper inside a clean jam jar and trickle a little water into the bottom of the jar to be absorbed by the paper.

Push two beans down between the side of the glass and the paper and put the lid on the jar. Check that the paper stays moist.

After a week or two the beans should grow a shoot and a root. When the first two leaves are grown, plant each bean in a pot.

Carrot tops

Cut the top 2 cm off a carrot with a tufty crown where the leaves were removed. Place this, cut side down, in a saucer of water. Keep the saucer topped up with water and watch carefully. You will not grow a carrot but a bushy plant with feathery leaves.

Try the tops of beetroot, parsnips, turnips . . .

Be careful that children do not put compost or pips into their mouths, or play with polythene bags.

SKITTLES

Cut strips of card about 2 cm wide and 8 cm long. Cut out funny faces from magazines and stick one on to each strip. Fold in half so they stand up well.
Use a toilet roll tube as a chute.
Position skittles and aim the chute.
Get some marbles or small balls ready and . . . roll 'em!

You do not need to knock down the skittles, only hit them to score.
How many can you score with six shots?

Try making a complete skittle family.

PAINTED PASTA

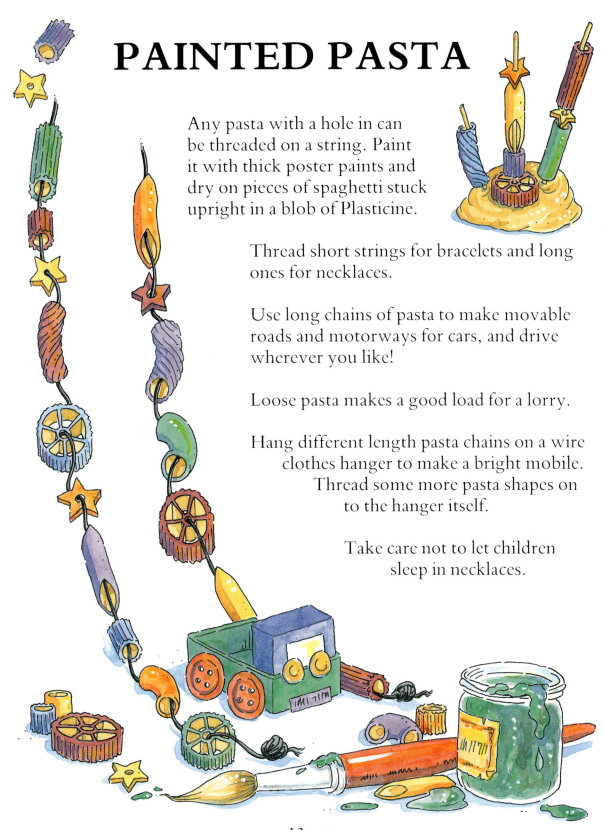

Any pasta with a hole in can be threaded on a string. Paint it with thick poster paints and dry on pieces of spaghetti stuck upright in a blob of Plasticine.

Thread short strings for bracelets and long ones for necklaces.

Use long chains of pasta to make movable roads and motorways for cars, and drive wherever you like!

Loose pasta makes a good load for a lorry.

Hang different length pasta chains on a wire clothes hanger to make a bright mobile. Thread some more pasta shapes on to the hanger itself.

Take care not to let children sleep in necklaces.

ROGUES' GALLERY

Use wallpaper lining paper, computer print-out paper or large single sheets taped together. Get the child to lie down very still on the paper and draw round her body. Then use felt pens, pencils or paints to draw in the face and colour the clothes for a life-size portrait.

Don't forget buttons, finger-nails, shoe-laces . . .

Try sticking wool hair on to the picture or painting imaginary clothes in crazy colours!

How tall am I?

Tape the picture to the child's bedroom door, with extra paper above it, and measure how fast she grows . . .

A SPINNING DICE

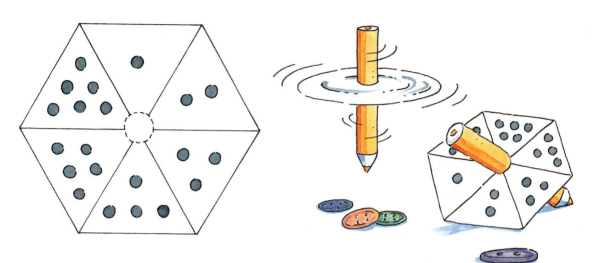

Copy or trace this six-sided shape on to card and cut out. Cut a pencil thick hole in the centre. Divide into segments and draw large spots in each segment, increasing from one to six. Poke a pencil through the hole and spin. The dice will always land on one segment and those are the spots to count.

 A game of dice

Each player takes a turn to spin the dice. The number tells him how many pieces of clothing he must put on – anything will do – socks, gloves, hats, jumpers, T-shirts, scarves . . . The winner is the last one still able to fit anything on!

Snakes and ladders (see pp. 16 and 17)

Two or more players take turns to spin the dice and move a button or counter as many squares as the dice shows. If you land on the bottom of a ladder climb up to the square at the top. If you land on the head of a snake slither down to the square at its tail. The first one to finish is the winner!

POM-POMS

Cut two identical circles of strong card the size you want your pom-pom to be. Cut a hole in each – not smaller than 3 cm in diameter. Put the two rings together and tie a ball of wool to them. Wind it through the hole and evenly round the rings until the hole is completely filled up.

Slip some scissors between the two pieces of card and cut round the outside edge to undo the wool. Be careful not to pull the strands out.

When they are all cut, tie a piece of strong wool between the two card rings and knot tightly. Cut the rings away and fluff out the pom-pom. The rings can be used again with the cuts taped up.

Try using lots of colours, or sparkly wool for Christmas decorations.

Try sticking or sewing felt eyes on to two pom-poms and stitching them on your gloves to make a pair of wriggly five-legged spiders!

LANTERNS

Take a rectangle of coloured stiff paper or card. Fold in half lengthways and cut slits along the edge, two thirds of the way through. Unfold, roll into a cylinder and tape together. Cut a strip of paper and attach at the top for a handle.

Try decorating the paper, before cutting, with finger or string printing, paints or pencils. Or, after cutting, dab with glue and sprinkle with glitter for a party decoration.

MAGIC PAINTINGS

Take a sheet of heavy paper and paint it all over in a swirl of bright colours. When it's dry, cover the paper completely with thick black wax crayon. Then scratch a pattern on the paper with something blunt such as a nail file and see the colours appear through the black, as if by magic!

Draw a pattern on a white sheet of paper with a white wax candle. Then paint over the paper in watercolour or poster paint using lots of bright colours. The pattern will magically appear through the paint!

CREEPY CRAWLIES

Slow smiley snail

Cut a long strip of stiff paper or card. Decorate on both sides. Make a sharp fold half way along and curl one half back on itself around a pencil. Fold the flat half at right angles for the body and cut a V-shape at the end.

Draw large bright eyes, cut them out and stick on to the head. Draw a smiley mouth underneath.

Make a family of slow slimy smiley snails.

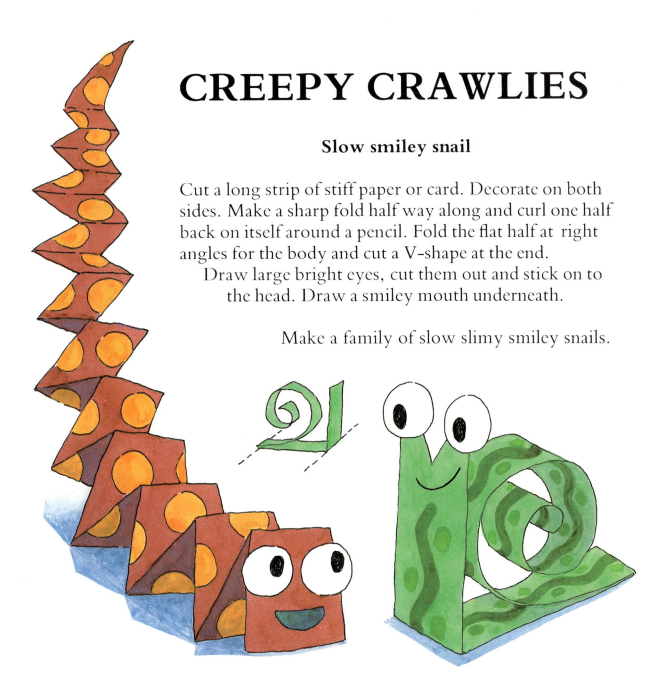

Crawly crinkle caterpillar

Cut a long strip of stiff paper or card so that it tapers to a point at the end. Decorate on both sides using pencils, paints or sticky shapes. Draw two large eyes. Cut them out and stick on to the face and draw a mouth underneath. Fold the paper concertina fashion – and then choose a name for your creepy crawly crinkle caterpillar!

SNAP!

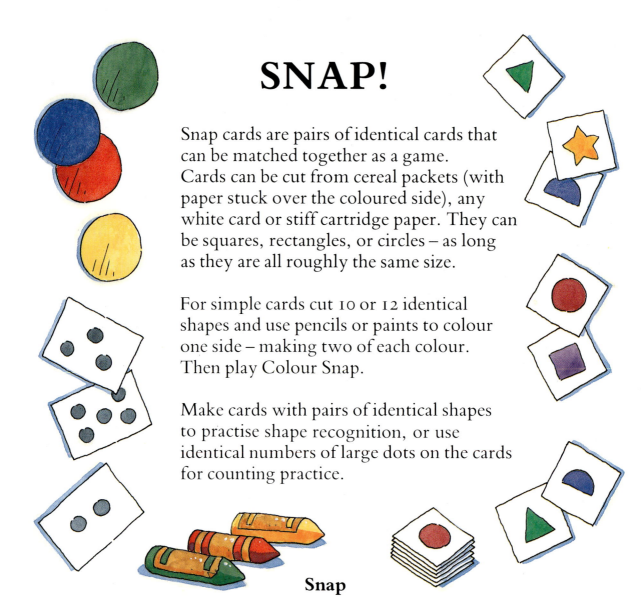

Snap cards are pairs of identical cards that can be matched together as a game. Cards can be cut from cereal packets (with paper stuck over the coloured side), any white card or stiff cartridge paper. They can be squares, rectangles, or circles – as long as they are all roughly the same size.

For simple cards cut 10 or 12 identical shapes and use pencils or paints to colour one side – making two of each colour. Then play Colour Snap.

Make cards with pairs of identical shapes to practise shape recognition, or use identical numbers of large dots on the cards for counting practice.

Snap

Deal the cards, picture side down, between players. Each shows a card in turn. When two show the same picture, the first player to shout SNAP! takes those cards. The winner is the player who takes all the cards.

Pairs

Spread out the cards, picture side down. Each player turns over two cards trying to find a pair – if he does he keeps them, if not he turns them back over and the next player has a go. When all the cards are gone, the player with the most pairs is the winner!

FLOUR PICTURES

Use a tea tray or baking tray. Spread a layer of flour to cover the base and then draw pictures and patterns with your finger in the flour. When the picture is finished shake the tray and draw something new!

Use currants or buttons for eyes and wheels . . .

FINGER AND FOOTPRINTS

Mix some thick paint and brush it on to an old sponge. Press a finger on the sponge and print on to paper.
Each finger will make a different shape – try the side of a little finger for tiny shapes, or the side of the whole hand curled up.
Use pencils or felt pens to add details to the prints.

Make a print of the whole hand. When the paint is dry draw faces, hair, bow-ties and jewellery on the fingers to make a family.

Lay a large sheet of paper on the floor with plenty of newspaper underneath. Put a little paint in the bottom of a washing-up bowl, take off shoes and socks and . . . make footprints!

Have soapy water and a towel to hand.

STRING PAINTING

Use parcel string, cord, hairy string, frayed string, thick wool, an odd shoe-lace . . .
Make up some thick poster paint and dip the string in. Let the excess paint drip off. Lay the string in curly swirls on to paper and then lift off to make a print.
Try different colours and a variety of strings.

Try folding a piece of paper in half then opening it flat. Lay painted string on one half, fold paper over and press lightly. Open and remove string to find a symmetrical pattern.

IT'S SEW EASY!

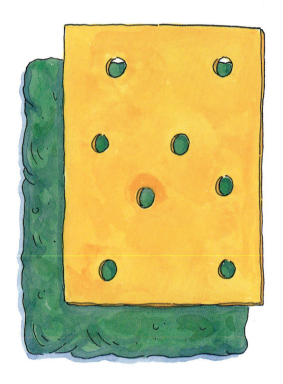

Use a piece of strong card or the back of a cereal packet. Cut into quarters. Roll out a piece of Plasticine to protect the table, lay the card on top and punch holes with a pencil.
Take a shoe-lace with a knot at one end and thread it through the holes to make lines, criss crosses and patterns.

Unthread cards to use again.

Use stripy laces and mix colours. Or use string with sticky tape around the end for easy threading.

Try drawing a simple picture on the card, punch holes around the outline and 'sew a picture'.

RUBBINGS

You can make a rubbing from anything that is flat with a bumpy or holey surface.
Try kitchen tiles or flooring with a rough or patterned surface.
Try different-shaped leaves, coins, scraps of net, the outline of stamps, paper doilies . . .
Use a pencil or crayon with thin paper for delicate rubbings and thick paper for rough surfaces.

A scrapbook

Make a colourful pattern of leaf rubbings on two sheets of paper and stick them on to the covers of a scrapbook. Add a label with your name and use it as a Nature Scrapbook. Stick in anything you find outside – pressed flowers, leaves, feathers, small seeds or pictures of the animals and birds you see.

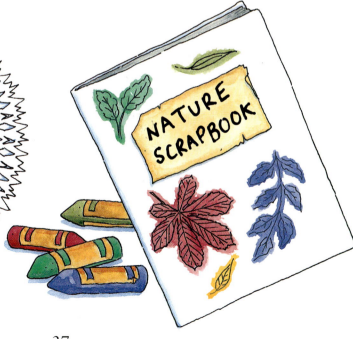

FEELING FANCY

A bracelet

Decorate a wide strip of strong paper with pencils, pens or paints then tape into a band. Stick on jewels of scrunched up tissue paper, shiny sweet wrappers or foil.

Rings

Make small bands of decorated paper. Add sticky shapes for jewels or flowers cut from magazines. Old mail order catalogues provide pictures of rings with gemstones.

A watch

Cut out a watch or clock face from a magazine and stick it on to a wide band of strong paper. Tape around the wrist.

A necklace

Cut a large decoration from a magazine – a butterfly, flower, teddy bear – or draw one. Tape it on to a long piece of wool, string or a coloured bootlace and tie a knot at the end.

Do not let small children sleep in necklaces.

PLASTICINE PRINTING

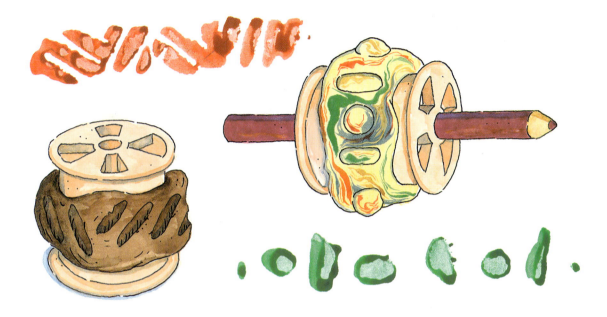

Roll a snake of Plasticine around a cotton reel. Stick small Plasticine shapes firmly on to roll or make marks with a pencil or fork. Put a pencil through the cotton reel and paint the Plasticine with poster paint. Roll it over paper to print a pattern. . .

Noughts and crosses

Use your Plasticine printer, with pencil or fork marks, to roll out a grid. One player is noughts and the other crosses. They take it in turns to make their mark in a square. The first to get a straight or diagonal line of three is the winner!

LET'S PRETEND...

To make an astronaut's helmet, mould papier mâché (see p. 32) on to a round balloon. When it is dry, pop and remove the balloon. Cut out a panel for the face and then cover in silver foil. Tape foil over shoes for moonboots...

A pirate wears a handkerchief knotted at the corners. Add a paper eye patch with wool taped on for tying. Try a swashbuckling moustache with eyebrow or kohl pencil, applied over cold cream.

A card cone can be painted black for a witch's or wizard's hat and decorated with silver foil shapes.
For the brim of a witch's hat cut a large painted circle with a centre hole to fit the cone through, and tape together. Stick straggly black wool inside the rim for hair.
Cut teeth out of a quarter of orange peel... and grin at someone!
A long-handled brush makes a perfect broomstick!

A crown made of card can be decorated with silver foil, glitter or coloured paper jewels. (Scraps of coloured paper can be cut from magazines.)
A blanket makes a royal cloak.

A brightly painted cone with pom-poms of cotton wool can be a clown's hat. Paint a section of an egg box red for a nose and tape wool at the sides for tying. Use face paints or make-up, applied over cold cream, for a smiley clown's face. Dress up in over-size clothes and shoes and . . . clown about!

A paper plate or a cylinder of card with holes for eyes and mouth can be . . . anything! Decorate with pencils, paints, tissue paper, scraps of fabric, glitter, sticky shapes, foil, straws, wool, string . . .
Tape wool to the sides of paper plates for tying. Add large ears and a trunk cut from paper for an elephant. Pipe cleaners make whiskers for cats. A scarf or sock can be safety-pinned on to trousers or skirt for a tail.

BITS AND BOBS

Useful sources of materials

Save cereal packets, shoe boxes, card stiffeners from new shirts or tights, old greetings cards, computer print-out paper, left over wallpaper or lining (a roll of lining paper from a wallpaper shop is an excellent cheap source of drawing paper), old wrapping paper, used envelopes opened out for drawing, old magazines or mail order catalogues for cut-outs, toilet rolls, cardboard tubes from foil or cling film, paper plates, tissue paper from packaging, wool, string and ribbon from presents . . .

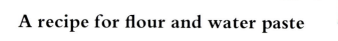

A recipe for flour and water paste

Mix water and flour to make a smooth runny sauce. Cook in a saucepan over medium heat, stirring constantly until mixture becomes gluey. More water makes a thin glue. More flour makes a thick paste. The glue sets further as it cools.

Papier mâché

Make up some thin flour and water paste – see above. Tear newspaper into small pieces – the size depends on the object used as a mould. Try a bowl or a cup for a simple mould. Apply a coat of paste to the mould and then cover evenly with newspaper. Apply more paste and paper until the papier mâché is at least ½ cm thick. Allow to dry thoroughly. Then gently pull the papier mâché away from the mould. Paint with thick poster paints.